Juneteenth
Celebrating the End of Slavery

The Rosen Publishing Group's
READING ROOM
Collection™

New York

Published in 2003 by The Rosen Publishing Group, Inc.
29 East 21st Street, New York, NY 10010

First Library Edition 2003

Book Design: Haley Wilson

Photo Credits: Cover, p. 1 © Mark Downey/Lucid Images/Picture Quest; pp. 4–5 © Bob Daemmrich/Stock Boston Inc./Picture Quest; pp. 6–7 © FPG International; pp. 8–9 © PhotoWorld/FPG International; pp. 10–11 © Corbis; p. 10 (General Gordon Granger) © Medford Historical Society Collection/Corbis; p. 13 © Owen Franken/Corbis; p. 15 © Kelly-Mooney Photography/Corbis; p. 17 © Annie Griffiths Belt/Corbis; pp. 18, 20 © Elizabeth Watt Photography/Food Stock America; p. 19 © Philip Gould/Corbis; p. 22 © John Kelly/The Image Bank.

Library of Congress Cataloging-in-Publication Data

Levy, Janey.
   Juneteenth : celebrating the end of slavery / Janey Levy.
      p. cm. — (The Rosen Publishing Group's reading room collection)
Summary: Explores the roots of the Juneteenth holiday that celebrates
the end of slavery in the United States.
   ISBN 0-8239-3711-9 (lib. bdg.)
   1. Juneteenth—Juvenile literature. 2. African
Americans—Texas—Galveston—Social life and customs—-Juvenile
literature. 3. Slaves—Emancipation—United States—Juvenile
literature. 4. African Americans—Anniversaries, etc—Juvenile
literature. 5. African Americans—Social life and customs—Juvenile
literature. 6. Galveston (Tex.)—Social life and customs—Juvenile
literature. [1. Juneteenth. 2. Slavery. 3. Holidays.] I. Title. II.
Series.
   F394.G2 L63 2003
   973.7'14—dc21
                              2001007997

Manufactured in the United States of America

For More Information
Electronic Village: Juneteenth
http://www.elecvillage.com/juneteen.htm

Kulture Zone – Kulture Kidz
http://www.kulturezone.com/kidz/index.html

Contents

Juneteenth
is celebrated in
many countries
around the world.

TEXAS

Galveston

4

What Is Juneteenth?

Juneteenth is the oldest known **celebration** of the ending of **slavery**. It began in Galveston, Texas, and spread across the United States. People celebrate Juneteenth as a special time to remember the past, honor freedom, and be together with family and friends.

Slavery in the United States

Slavery was a terrible system in which one group of people "owned" another. **Slaves** were an important part of life on the large **plantations** in the southern states.

Farmers used slaves to plant, tend, and **harvest** the crops because that was cheaper than paying someone to do the work. Slaves were not treated well and had no freedom.

Grown-ups and children were taken by force from their homes in Africa and brought to America to work as slaves.

"All Slaves Are Free"

General Gordon Granger was a leader in the Northern army. He became the governor of Texas after the Civil War. On June 19, 1865, he arrived in Galveston, Texas, with the news that the war was over and the North had won. He read a special **announcement** that said "all slaves are free" and all people now had equal rights. As soon as the freed slaves heard this, they began to celebrate.

General Gordon Granger

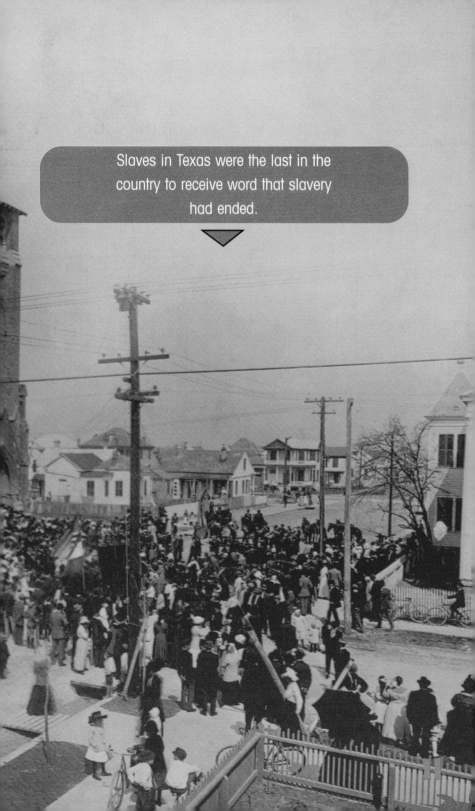

The First Juneteenth

The **tradition** of Juneteenth began on the evening of June 19, 1865, when thousands of freed slaves filled the streets of Galveston, Texas. They sang, danced, and prayed to celebrate their new freedom. They also prepared special foods. They **barbecued** (BAR-bih-kyud) meat, cooking it over fires built in holes in the ground that were lined with rocks.

"Barbecue" comes from a Native American word that means "to cook over coals." Barbecue is still a part of many Juneteenth celebrations.

The Clothes of Freedom

Clothes were an important part of early Juneteenth celebrations. During slavery there were laws that told slaves what they could wear and what they couldn't wear. When slaves first learned that they had been set free, many threw away their slave clothes. They put on new clothes like the ones their owners had worn to show that they were now free and had equal rights.

Clothes are still an important part of Juneteenth celebrations today. People often wear bright colors and patterns much like those worn in Africa.

Juneteenth Traditions

Many activities besides dance, song, food, and prayer have become traditions at Juneteenth celebrations. Sometimes there are parades. Often the Emancipation Proclamation is read. Education is considered important, so there are educational speeches. People can also fish and play games like baseball. Elders are often asked to share their memories of things that happened in the past.

Juneteenth is a special time to be together with family and friends.

Special Foods

Juneteenth celebrations include foods that were a traditional part of plantation life, such as barbecued meat, **collard greens**, sweet potatoes, corn bread, and pecan pie. Many red foods are prepared to remind people of the blood spilled during the Civil War. There are red drinks, red barbecue **sauce**, and a special red "emancipation" cake.

There is always plenty of food during a Juneteenth celebration. Everyone brings a special dish.

Recipe for Emancipation Cake

Have a grown-up help make this cake.

You will need:

2 cups cake flour
3 tablespoons unsweetened cocoa powder
2 teaspoons baking powder
1 teaspoon salt
3/4 cup (1 1/2 sticks) butter, softened
1 3/4 cups sugar
4 large eggs
1 cup milk
3 teaspoons red food coloring*
1 teaspoon vanilla extract

Prepared vanilla frosting

How to do it:

Preheat the oven to 350 degrees. Use two nonstick 9-inch cake pans, or grease and flour two regular 9-inch cake pans. In a large bowl, stir together the flour, cocoa, baking powder, and salt. In another large bowl, mix together the butter and sugar until light and fluffy. Beat in the eggs one at a time. In a small bowl, combine the milk, food coloring, and vanilla. Mix everything together. Pour the batter into the cake pans and bake for 30 to 35 minutes. Take the cakes out of the oven. Let them cool for 5 minutes, then remove them from the pans. When they are completely cool, frost one of the cakes with the vanilla frosting. Place the other cake on top and frost the entire cake.

* Make sure that no one is allergic to red food coloring.

Honoring Freedom for All

Like the Fourth of July, Juneteenth is a day for all Americans to celebrate freedom and equal rights for all. In 1980, Texas became the first state to make Juneteenth an official state holiday. Many other states also honor this day. Perhaps this important day will soon become an official holiday throughout the United States.

Glossary

American Civil War   A war between the Northern states and the Southern states that lasted from 1861 to 1865.

announcement   An official statement made to the public about something.

barbecue   To cook meat over an open fire.

celebration   A special event honoring something important.

collard greens   The leaves of a vegetable that grows in the South.

harvest   To gather crops after they have grown.

plantation   A large farm owned by one family and worked by the people who live on the land.

sauce   A thick liquid poured over food to give it extra taste.

slave   A person who is "owned" by another person.

slavery   The unfair system of being "owned" by someone else and having to work for them.

tradition   Something that has been done a certain way for a long time by a group of people.

Index

B

barbecue(d), 12, 18

C

Civil War, 8, 10, 18

clothes, 14

E

education(al), 16

elders, 16

"emancipation"
   cake, 18, 20, 21

Emancipation
   Proclamation, 9, 16

equal rights, 10, 14, 22

F

family and friends, 5

free(dom), 5, 7, 9, 10, 12, 14, 22

G

Galveston, Texas, 5, 10, 12

games, 16

Granger, General Gordon, 10

L

Lincoln, Abraham, 9

N

North, 8, 9, 10

P

plantation(s), 6, 18

R

red foods, 18

S

slavery, 5, 6, 8, 9, 14

slave(s), 6, 7, 9, 10, 12, 14

South, 8